THE POWER OF MEDIATION

Somto Ubezonu, Ph.D.

Mediator

(Essays and Articles on Mediations by Mediators with at least five years experience)

Compiled and Prepared by:

Somto Ubezonu, Ph.D.
Certified Mediator/Real Estate Investor

THE POWER OF MEDIATION

PENDIUM
PUBLISHING HOUSE
514-201 DANIELS STREET
RALEIGH, NC 27605

For information, please visit our Web site at
www.pendiumpublishing.com

PENDIUM Publishing and its logo
are registered trademarks.

The Power of Mediation
By Somto Ubezonu, Ph.D.

Copyright © Somto Ubezonu, Ph.D., 2013
All Rights Reserved.

ISBN: 978-1-936513-76-5

PUBLISHER'S NOTE

Without limiting the rights under the copyright reserved above, no part of this publication may be reproduced, stored in or introduced into a retrieval system, or transmitted, in any form, or by any means (electronic, mechanical, photocopying, recording, or otherwise), without the prior written permission of both the copyright owner and the above publisher of this book.

If you purchased this book without a cover you should be aware that the book is stolen property. It was reported as "unsold and destroyed" to the publisher and neither the author nor the publisher has received any payment for this "stripped book."

This book is printed on acid-free paper.

DEDICATION

This book is dedicated to those who work diligently to resolve conflicts arising among individuals. Also, it is dedicated to men and women of God that intervene in resolving disputes within and out of their congregations.

Table of Contents

Dedication i

Introduction v

Chapter 1: Litigate Or Mediate?:
Mediation As An Alternative To Lawsuits 1

Chapter 2: Mediation: A Process To Regain
Control of Your Life 6

Chapter 3: What Does A Mediator Do? 11

Chapter 4: Mediator Neutrality: How is it possible? 14

Chapter 5: Why Mediation Works 22

Chapter 6: All You Need To Know About Mediation
But Didn't Know To Ask-A Parachute For
Parties In Litigation! 28

INTRODUCTION

What Mediation is All About

Mediation is a process for resolving disputes. It is where a neutral person (mediator) helps conflicting parties to have a conversation to jointly resolve their differences. Mediations can help communities, organizations, and individuals survive their conflicts.

The American Heritage Dictionary defined mediation as an attempt to bring about a peaceful settlement between disputants through the intervention of a neutral party.

The purpose of putting these articles together is to create awareness and let people know that there is an alternative to litigating a case which is mediation. I decided to put these articles together because I plan to be doing more mediations. As of the time I am working on this book, I have been a Certified Mediator for almost three years.

During the process of the mediation, some things do transpire. The mediator guides the process but does not make a decision on who is right or wrong, but should have a clear understanding of both sides' arguments. The mediator is there to help the parties work towards an outcome that best satisfies everyone. The mediator has the responsibility to provide a conducive environment for people to talk freely, listen and be able to resolve their differences.

There are some qualities that I think that a mediator should have. He or she should be neutral, independent, unbiased, patient, and diligent. He should further use wisdom and treat all disputes with the same seriousness and concern.

Does Mediation Really Work

Mediation really works because people get a chance to tell each other their frustrations, tell each other how they feel and agree on an amicable way to resolve the dispute. It provides the opportunity for people to have a face to face conversation and speak honestly to each other.

During the process of the mediation, disputants are free to say whatever that bothers them without any restriction. Mediation also works because it does not take a long time to resolve a conflict and does not cost too much money unlike a litigation which may cost a lot of money and may be taking a lot of time to resolve.

Mediation can help lessen some frictions and misunderstandings. Both parties are always eager to resolve the conflicts as soon as possible.

Finally, as a Christian, I always reference God in anything that I do. Calling on the good Lord to be in charge and take control of any situation. Before I start to mediate a dispute, I pray to God to give me Divine guidance.

Prayer is a religious exercise. We pray because we are

imperfect human beings. If the Bible scriptures can be used during mediation, it will make a lot of difference and give wisdom to the mediation process. The more I read the Bible, the more I feel it provides the facts we need to manage the disputes and conflicts that come our way.

In the final analysis, if a mediator can always utilize the Bible scriptures during the process of mediations, that would be great. In the book of Colossians—3:13: The Bible says "bearing with one another, and forgiving one another, if anyone has a complaint against another, even as Christ forgave you, so you also must do." Also in Proverbs —20:13: The Bible also says that "it is honorable for a man to stop striving, since any fool can start a quarrel."

By: Somto Ubezonu, Ph.D.
    Certified Mediator
    To order more copies of this book, please contact: Dr. Somto Ubezonu @
    (919) 618-0128 or email: ubezfoundations@yahoo.com

Chapter 1

Litigate Or Mediate?: Mediation As An Alternative To Lawsuits

What Is Mediation?

One often hears the term "mediation" in connection with resolution of disputes which have already become lawsuits, and occasionally, before those lawsuits are filed. Mediation is a process by which a neutral third party called a mediator hears a dispute between two or more parties who can mediate and attempts to help the parties settle their disputes without judging the merits of the case. The term "mediation" is often confused with the term "arbitration." Arbitration is another form of dispute resolution by a third party (as opposed to a trial before a judge or jury): the Arbitrator listens to the evidence presented by each party and then makes a judgment as to who is responsible for the claimant's damages, and how much the responsible person must pay to the claimant, if any payment is due.

Who Can Mediate A Case?

Mediators range in training from practicing attorneys, retired judges or other professionals to highly trained mediators who work full or part time in the specialized field of mediation. The right mediator for your case is one who demonstrates overriding neutrality in evaluating and resolving your case. The effective mediator will help the parties recognize the strengths and weaknesses of both sides' case, so that at the end of mediation both parties are reasonably satisfied with the outcome. The effective mediator will also help parties consider the risks and costs of resolving a dispute before a judge or jury, without necessarily meeting the expectations of either party.

Mediate, Or Litigate?

Ninety-five percent of cases filed in the California court system settle before trial. Some settle early others settle on the eve of trial or as close as after a jury is picked. The difference between the former and the latter is the amount of money and time a party will spend in getting from one point to the other. Depending on the type of case, the cost could range from hundreds to several thousands of dollars. Often, the costs are not recovered at the time of settlement. Thus both parties bear their own burden of costs.

Mediating a case before a lawsuit is filed enables the parties to present their case to a mutually selected neutral person (or in some cases two persons as co-mediators) before any money is spent on litigation. Many times the simple process of telling one's story to a neutral willing to listen will take the parties a long way toward settlement.

The cost of mediating a case (which can be as little as a few hundred dollars, or as much as several thousand dollars per day) is minimal compared to the cost incurred through the life of a lawsuit.

Will The Court Make Me Mediate?

In some cases, contracts between the parties require that a case be mediated and/or arbitrated. This often occurs in medical malpractice actions, construction contracts, and real estate purchase agreement. In some cases statues require pre-litigation mediation or alternative dispute resolution, such as in most types of home owners association disputes. The excessive backlog in court calendars makes mediation an attractive alternative in other types of cases, resulting in the resolution of disputes in a timely manner, and avoiding the painstaking experience of costly litigation lasting up to five years.

How Do I Start The Mediation Process?

If you have a dispute with another person or business, which you want resolved, you can first propose to the other side to mediate the case. If you are uncomfortable with that option, then you can make the first call to the mediator and ask the mediator to approach the other side with the invitation to mediate. A well-trained mediator can effectively maintain his or her neutrality during this process.

If you are not familiar with any mediators, you can call the local court and ask for potential mediators, or you can call your local bar association which often has a panel of mediators. Other possible sources are the Internet, as well as private mediation companies.

Select a mediator who has some familiarity with the area of law of your dispute (i.e., home owners association, family law, etc.) and someone in your geographic area. Ask the mediator what his or her fees are, and how much time he or she will allocate to your dispute. A good mediator will commit as much time as is necessary to help you resolve your dispute.

What If Mediation Does Not Settle My Case?

In most states, what takes place in mediation is confidential. For example, in California, the mediator cannot be forced to testify at trail as to what was said in a mediation hearing. Any offers made during the mediation process, and any concessions made, are confidential if the case doesn't settle. Of course, certain limitations do exist in connection with protecting others from danger or imminent harm, or in connection with illegal activities. But, parties to most typical disputes over money or negligent conduct are generally protected by laws of confidentiality.

What Is The Secret To A Successful Mediation?

The mediation process is as successful as the willingness of the parties to participate in good faith to reach a settlement. A good mediator will work with the parties until he or she determines that a settlement cannot be reached at the time. Parties who consider what they have learned during the mediation process often reach a settlement after the hearing in order to avoid spending precious time and additional funds which may never be recovered at trial.

By: Adrinne Krikorian
   An Administrative Law Judge.

   An experience mediator and arbitrator.
   Also, and adjunct professor at Loyola Law School in Los Angeles.

Chapter 2

Mediation: A Process To Regain Control of Your Life

Are you weary of trying to solve the pressing conflicts in your life through long drawn out legal battles?

Does the thought of a judge, or another person of authority, dictating the resolution of your problems, despite your desires, bother you?

Are you concerned about the prospects of paying lawyer's fees ranging from $150 to $300 per hour for the many hours it takes to process a claim through the court system?

If you answered "no" to all the above questions, do not read any further. However, if you want to regain control of your life, read on.

Regain Control, Through Direct Involvement

Mediation provides a method for people with disputes or conflicts to exercise their own choices and discretion and to regain a sense of control over their lives in resolving disputes.

It is a means by which you can be an active participant in the decision making process and have direct involvements in the determination of your destiny. In the informal setting of mediation, the parties are given the opportunity to express their emotions and by searching for the identity of their true interests, to ease their emotional turmoil. Instead of having a decision forced upon the parties to a dispute, mediation provides the mechanism for the parties to craft their own decisions. Once a mutually acceptable agreement is reached, the parties breathe easier and are able to end the emotional turmoil that would continue to plague them for an unknown time into the future while awaiting resolve of their case through litigation.

Because of the voluntary nature of mediation, and the direct involvement of the parties at every step of the proceeding, the process is totally different from the established methods of resolving disputes through litigation. Contrasted with the formality of litigation, mediation is informal and encourages the open exchange of discussion between the parties. As opposed to the limited number of options available in litigation, mediation provides the ability for creative resolution of problems, molded to fit the particular needs of the parties. In addition to tailoring agreements to the particular circumstances of the parties, mediation remains, at all times, a confidential process, thus further fostering a restoration of prior good relationships.

The Rush To the Courthouse
The Mindset of Our Times

As a lawyer who has specialized in civil litigation in the United States for over 35 years, I have personally witnessed the evolution of a mindset that propels people to the court house for every real or imagined wrong. As the rush to litigation has grown, the sphere of individual patience has finished. Rather than attempting to calmly discuss each other's feelings and determine the driving force behind the dispute, there is a rush to the lawyer's office. By these comments, I do not mean to demean the valuable services provided by lawyers to their clients. Unfortunately, the lawyer sometimes gets caught up in the client's insistence that the lawyer be his/her "mouthpiece", including mimicking the emotions of the client. There then develops a point in the litigation process in which the process becomes self sustaining (a goal in and of itself), leaving little hope for early peaceful resolution.

Analyze The Gamble In Litigation
What Is The Real risk Of Your Gamble?

As is the case with people who gamble, most litigants believe that they have a strong likelihood of winning in court. It is interesting for the mediator to ask the parties, after listening to their prediction of the outcome they believe they are entitled to, if their attorneys are prepared to guarantee those outcomes. In the same vein, the parties need to ask themselves, if there are any guarantees that the result won't be one-half or double, or one fourth or quadruplet the expectations.

What Are The Costs Of The Gamble?

The disputants need to factor in the amount it may cost to find out if they are right, and whether there is any assurance that such cost won't be double or more. In mediation, the parties have better control of the costs, as they are involved in all steps of the process. They don't have to suffer the orders of a court requiring their attorneys to spend valuable time and money submitting lengthy legal documents.

Time Needed To See If The Gamble Was Correct

The parties need to get realistic grip on how long it will take to find out if they were correct in their guess as to the outcome. The average litigation can take years. By contrast, most mediations can be completed in a matter of weeks or months.

Do You Really Want To Abdicate Control?

After dealing with all of those questions, if the litigation process continues, the parties have abdicated their control to a judge, over whom they have no control. Isn't a negotiated settlement a better alternative?

Peace And Harmony Is Within Our Reach

Given the above, does it not make more sense to take a step back and regain control of your life by a proven method of alternative dispute resolution voluntary mediation? Mediation is the voluntary process where a neutral, impartial person, acceptable to all parties of a dispute, helps the parties to reach a mutually acceptable agreement to mend their dispute. That means that the parties choose to participate by their own free will and freely reach a settlement of their dispute. Mediation is a part of the negotiation process, but is not the imposition on parties to a dispute of a 3rd party to make decisions for them. The goal of the mediator is to not only help the parties reconcile their present areas of controversy, but by identifying their interests, to look to the future and through an exchange of mutually acceptable promises that the parties feel meet their personal standards of fairness. In contrast, with litigation, in a mediation, all sides to the dispute have a greater opportunity to walk away as winners.

Through the confidential and voluntary process, you will take an active role in the control and resolution of your problems. An agreement reached will allow all parties to walk away with their heads held high, as winners not just in the resolve of their problems, but in life. Peace and harmony is an attainable goal, at the financial and emotional cost which is far less than what will be spent in protracted litigation.

BY: Nathan Davidovich
Successful Trial Attorney with more than 15 years in mediation

Chapter 3

What Does A Mediator Do?

Okay, we know you can't make decisions. We know you don't issue orders. ('I'm not a judge or an arbitrator, blah, blah.') We know you can't take sides, must always remain neutral. And we know you can't give legal advice. And then you tell us mediation is a consensual process. Bummer. Now the other side can walk at will!

"So, what the hell DO you do?"

Oh, you've never said this in so many words, but we've read your minds and understand your frustration. In many cases, you'd like the mediator to play judge and settle the matter once and for all, right?

The problem is the law and regulations covering the conduct of mediators and process of mediation do not allow us to do these things, and it's well they do not.

Mediation is your process, not the mediator's. Decisions are yours and your client's to make, and mediation is the only forum in which you have complete control over decision making by or on behalf of your client. And, as much as you'd like the mediator to side with you, you don't really want this to happen, 'cause in a given case how would you know which side he or she actually is on, hmm?

And, finally, the rendering of legal advice is the job of the attorney representing the client. Ask for our opinion and we'll give it to you the best we can. But don't expect unsolicited advice. In the first place, you might resent it, professional pride being what it is, and, secondly, how would opposing counsel feel about our giving you favorable advice or reminding you of some legal principle you may have overlooked? He'll think, hmm, smells of bias.

So, what DO we do?

Well, first and foremost, we give you a hard time or try to. We ask you questions you probably don't want us to ask or have forgotten to ask yourself or your client, or have forgotten the answers to. We call them "reality checks."

We'll ask you and your client what it is you're really looking for in a settlement. We do this as much for your benefit, to be sure you are clear about your expectations, as for ours in helping you reach that goal.

We'll bore you with clichés that, while you've heard them ad nauseam, are probably quite original to your clients and frequently do serve to refine the objectives in steering parties toward a resolution.

We remind you to look at the big picture and not focus on inconsequential legal or factual issues. They merely distract you from the key issues and your settlement goal.

We tell you and your client (just in case it hasn't been discussed in recent weeks or months) trials are expensive, stressful, take time and that their outcomes are terribly uncertain.

While subtle and often not appreciated, by separating the parties in breakout or caucus sessions, we are able to control heated emotions that can frustrate a settlement and to keep folks focused on their interests rather than their positions.

And, finally, we try to make the point that an amicable settlement, while not always satisfactory to either side, is the best of all worlds and a win-win for both sides.

Oh, also, occasionally, we'll share the latest good joke with you, even if it's not always worth the cost of admission.

By: Edwards Ahrens
    A certified mediator with many years experience. Has been a member of the Florida Bar since 1970

Chapter 4

Mediator Neutrality: How is it possible?

How could a mediator be neutral about your situation when you are getting divorced? Surely one of you is right and the other is wrong. If you know in your bones and all of your friends agree that you are right, you may think that mediation would not make sense for you, because you don't want to compromise.

First of all let me reassure you that you won't agree to anything in mediation that you don't want to agree to! But something happens in mediation that changes people's goals and outlook. I don't ask my clients to agree with each other just to make an honest effort to understand each other. And to accomplish that, it turns out that mediator neutrality is one of the most valuable and powerful tools I have.

If I really understand how you are feeling, what the experience has done to you, what this means for you, the challenges that you are facing as you try to restructure your life then I can help your spouse understand these things. And I can make sure that the agreement that we put together takes care of you and your needs.

Mediator Neutrality: How is it possible?

The theory underlying our adversarial legal system, is that each person will hire a bright, skilled warrior who will see the situation completely from the perspective of the client, and then present the strongest case possible to the judge. The judge will get the best information from each side, but will be neutral. The judge will see the situation from above and will render a decision which metes out justice and wisdom.

Sadly, because of our overloaded and burdened court system, most judges do not have the time to get to know the people behind the case-load. People who go through the court system often end up feeling that they did not have their story heard by the judge, and that they were not given a chance to speak.

Mediation will give you that chance and you are the best person to speak about your life and your needs. No expert knows your life as well as you and your spouse do, In truth, no hired expert will care as much as you do because only you and your family will live with the agreement you make, You are the people who are in the best position to decide what should happen with your family, your possessions, and with your divorce.

As a mediator, I will not act as a judge, in that I will not make decisions FOR you but I will act as a judge in that I will remain neutral. I will do my best to listen to everything that each of you need to say, and I will ask questions to make sure that we have all of the information we need. If one person needs additional information, I will help to brainstorm to figure out how to get the information to that person. He or she might need the assistance of an accountant, a financial planner, or an attorney, before feeling confident enough to evaluate offers that are on the table or have enough background information to make decisions.

I will use all of the tools I have to make sure that each person HEARS the other. There is always miscommunication between divorcing people, but a neutral mediator can help to improve the communication to make sure that you understand where the other is coming from, and why you believe the proposed result is right. You don't have to agree with each other but it helps to understand why you disagree.

That is the theory. How does it work in practice? How is it possible to be on both people's sides, when they are in a conflict?

Anice and Marshall came to me for divorce mediation. Anice expressed her thoughts clearly. She loved Marshall passionately and still believed that he was the love of her life. She had made a commitment to him which, to her, meant that she would stay with him no matter what. She told me that Marshall had had other affairs in the past, and had always returned to his commitment to her. "How do I know that this time you are serious?" She asked him. "What makes you think that, 3 months from now, you won't change your mind again and come back to me?"

The couple had recently purchased a house. Anice said, "Why did you buy this house with me if you wanted to get out of the relationship?" The couple had greatly disparate incomes, and although Anice had been the motivating force behind their buying their home, she was not at the present time able to figure out how to pay the expenses of the house by herself.

I could have felt that Anice was "right," and Marshall a lousy toad. She was the one with commitment and vision, she felt sure that this marriage was the right thing and was able to stick with her husband through thick and thin. She planned and worked to enable them to buy a home. And after this loyalty, what was her reward? Constant betrayal, multiple affairs!

Then Marshall told me about his experience. He spoke eloquently about his need to move on from a relationship which felt stagnant to him, and from which he could no longer derive any sense of intimacy or romance. He was very grateful to Anice for all the love and support he had gotten from her, and the achievements he accomplished because of her support. But for a long time he felt that there were something missing. This feeling drove him to seek outside relationships, even though he had derived from Anice love such as he had never before experienced in his life.

At the present time, he felt stifled by the relationship. He felt responsible for Anice. He was aware that she wasn't able to earn as much money as he could earn, and he felt trapped. Although he felt platonic love and respect for Anice, he had a new girlfriend. For Marshall, the 12 year relationship had evolved into a friendship.

After hearing Marshall, I felt his pain. I felt how Anice's willingness to stay in a relationship with a man who was sleeping with another woman made Marshall feel trapped.

He saw her as a crazy woman who had no self respect, who would live with him even though he rejected her.

In truth, I felt great empathy for both Anice and Marshall. Through my understanding of them, I was able to sympathize with Anice, who felt deeply committed to this man, and hurt every time he told her that he still loved her and who felt that she would have stayed with him no matter what happened, even if he had outside relationships.

I felt empathy for Marshall, who expressed that his marriage, through it had endured for 12 years, had never completely fulfilled him. He felt an excitement at the chance to break free and try again in a new relationship form something that felt more healthy and fulfilling and less co-dependent and suffocating than his relationship with Anice.

My Job, now was to do my best to increase their understanding of each other. Marshall had a better understanding of how Anice felt than she had of his point of view. Once understanding improved, they would be ready to negotiate the fairest way for them to divide their house and their possessions.

Anice had to confront the reality that Marshall wanted a divorce. When I helped her to accept this, she was able to negotiate alimony for a period of time, so that she could keep the house and eventually become self-sufficient. Marshall saw the alimony as a way to buy his freedom, and it was a great relief to him to be able to do that. They both were satisfied with the terms and their divorce agreement was completed.

Mediator Neutrality: How is it possible?

Children perceive their parents neutrally during a divorce. As much as you might want your child to side with you against the other parent it won't happen and it shouldn't happen. A child will never thank you for taking away his mother or father. The children each contain a little bit of each parent, and they are able intuitively to understand both parents' points-of-view. The children understand the limitations and strengths of both their parents and love them.

I can think of many cases where I had deep empathy with both people, and could see both their sides. I had a case where the marriage was breaking up because the woman was a lesbian. I empathized with the husband. Allen, who, in his early 50's had to leave his beautiful house. He had to rethink his whole life with Marge, in light of these changes in her outlook. He had believed he'd had an OK marriage. He didn't want a new life, but the old one had been snatched from him.

Marge was able to communicate to me the excitement and liberation she felt as she embarked on her new life. She showed me that something had always felt wrong" in her life, and now, for the first time she didn't have that feeling.

Marge came to mediation believing that she had embarked on a course of self-discovery. But during our sessions, she came to a new understanding of how this journey had affected Allen. She ended up giving him a more generous financial settlement, partly to assuage her guilt, and partly to help Allen to also feel that he was getting an opportunity to embark on a new life that might hold some promise, excitement, even happiness not present in their old one.

The truth is that it is never simple to determine why a marriage ends. Something was probably always lacking in Allen and Marge's marriage. Why didn't Allen see that? Why didn't Marge know earlier? The end of the marriage is created by both, as the beginning was created by both.

My challenge is always to understand both people. In another case, the husband, Brad, went out to get a newspaper one Sunday morning and did not come back for 3 days. He left Helen with 2 young children, without even a note. I could imagine her anguish, and the fear of the children. But during our sessions, I could see that Helen never let Brad speak!! I'm not saying that what he did was right, only that I understand that he did the best he could and that something drove him to do this terrible thing. Something that he felt had been equally awful had been done to him or he would not have done this to her.

And that is probably the crux. I do believe that most of us are trying the best we can to make our way through this life. We try not to hurt the people we love, or have loved. And we do our best. But we are imperfect creatures, so we do not always succeed. We are hurt and we lash out and the other may not know that he/she has hurt us. Through my understanding, I can often help people to forgive themselves and each other which will help them to move forward into their new lives post-divorce.

Divorce raises all kinds of hurdles, as you restructure and begin to figure out your new life and also raises all kinds of complex emotions. When you are navigating the maze of these changes, the last thing you might want to hear is that your spouse's position has some validity. (And that is one of the appeals of the adversarial system. When you are hurt, angry and shaken up, who would not want to hire an experienced warrior, who will tell you that you are right and that your evil spouse should make amends usually monetary to avenge these wrongs?)

These feelings are especially intense where the impetus for the breakup of the marriage is a situation with deep emotional effect for example, where one person has a new lover, or where one person walked out on the other very suddenly and without warning. The "right" spouse might find that the new identity as a wronged person becomes intensely compelling and attractive.

The answer is that neutrality will bring you closer to the truth, and will help you to move on with your life.

By: Rachel Fishman Green, Esq.
    An attorney with six years of experience as a mediator

CHAPTER 5

Why Mediation Works

We are in the midst of a litigation crisis. The high cost and long delays associated with the trial of civil matters often make litigation an impractical method of resolving disputes. It is not uncommon for the attorney's fees, expert witness fees, jury fees, court reporter fees and other related costs to exceed the amount in dispute. Parties increasingly find that they are spending more to litigate than the cost to settle the matter.

What Is Mediation?

Mediation is a process for resolving disputes by which an independent mediator assists the parties in reaching a mutually satisfactory settlement. It is an extension of the parties own negotiations and is sometimes referred to as a "supercharged negotiation."

A mediation session involves a discussion of the dispute by the parties, as opposed to the formal presentation of witnesses and evidence such that takes place in a trial or arbitration. The session will normally be attended only by the mediator, the parties and their attorneys. Because of the informality of the process, mediation can usually be completed in a day or less.

The mediation process is entirely voluntary and nonbinding. The mediator has no power to render a decision or to force the parties to accept a settlement. Rather, the mediator's role is to assist their negotiations by identifying obstacles to settlement and developing strategies for overcoming them.

A mediation session is private and confidential. It is normally held in a private office or meeting room and no public record is made of the proceedings. If no settlement is reached, any statements during the proceedings are inadmissible as evidence in any subsequent litigation.

A mediation session typically begins with a joint meeting of the parties, their attorneys and in some cases, insurance company representatives. The mediator first explains the format and discusses the confidential and nonbinding nature of the proceedings. The mediator will then ask the attorneys for each of the parties to make a presentation of their case, identifying the issues in dispute.

Following the joint meeting, the mediator will usually separate the parties and begin meeting with them in a series of private confidential meetings called "caucuses". In these caucuses, the mediator works with each of the parties to analyze their case and develop options for settlement. Normally the mediator will caucus numerous times with both sides until the case either settles or it becomes apparent that settlement will not be reached.

Mediation is different from an arbitration in that the mediator does not render a decision. Instead mediation allows the parties to make their own decisions and fashion their own settlement. The mediator generally doesn't make recommendations but rather, allows the parties to make their own decisions based on a realistic analysis of their case.

Why Mediation Works

The American Arbitration Association reports that over 85% of all mediations result in a settlement. This is true even where all prior attempts at settlement have failed, where the parties are pessimistic about the prospects of settlement, and where the parties have spent substantial amounts of time and money preparing for a trial. So why does mediation work, when the parties have been unable to settle the case themselves? There are a number of reasons.

First, negotiations between parties or their attorneys may never take place without the assistance of a third party mediator. Attorneys often fear that the making of any "reasonable" settlement offer will be taken as a sign of weakness or will be used by the other side as the starting point for the next round of negotiations. Mediation provides a safe environment for negotiation because the mediator can control and direct the communications. In this fashion, unproductive discussions can be avoided and concessions or proposals will be communicated only if they are likely to lead to a settlement.

Second, in those cases where some negotiations have taken place, they are often unsuccessful because the parties lack essential negotiation skills. Attorneys are often more interested in posturing, than in resolving disputes. As a result, they often employ hard bargaining tactics which emphasize the differences in their positions rather than seeking a common ground for settlement. Since the mediator's job is to keep the parties focused on exploring productive avenue to settlement, posturing and hard bargaining are often reduced or eliminated.

Third, mediation provides the opportunity for all parties to meet at the bargaining table for the express purpose of discussing settlement. All decision-makers necessary to resolve a problem are normally present. These decision-makers, who otherwise may be unavailable or distracted by other business matters, are able to focus their entire attention on reaching a settlement.

Fourth, during the mediation session, each party is given the opportunity to directly educate and influence their opponents in the opening presentation. Important issues can be emphasized and facts can be presented in a more favorable light. Also, the intensity of a party's feelings or emotions can be conveyed. As a result, the mediation session normally provided each side with a more realistic view of the opposing position (one not filtered through lawyers) and often results in the consideration of settlement proposals that otherwise would have been rejected.

Fifth, mediation allows each side to "test market" a settlement proposal by privately conveying the proposal to the mediation in a caucus. Unless authorized to do so, the mediator will not convey the proposal to the other party. The mediator will, however, be able to receive confidential proposals from the other side. As a consequence, the mediator will be able to determine whether a proposal is feasible without actually disclosing it to the other side. This allows each side to fully explore settlement options without negotiating against themselves or appearing to "give in".

Sixth, mediation offers each party a "realistic" look at their case and what results they are likely to achieve in court or arbitration. As the parties become clear on what they can realistically expect to achieve, their positions on settlement become more reasonable and flexible.

Seventh, mediation assists the parties in developing options for settlement. The more options that are developed, the greater the chances of success. Experience demonstrates that attorneys often excel in developing facts that support their positions but bog down when it comes to developing settlement options. The Mediator can assist the parties to clarify their real objective and to consider alternatives that might be overlooked by attorney engaged in battle,

Conclusion

The bottom line is that mediation works! It works because it brings all necessary parties to the bargaining table where they can "realistically" evaluate their positions and safely explore settlement options. I work in settling over 85% of the cases in which it is utilized, including those where the parties have been unable or unwilling to negotiate, or have taken unrealistic or intransigent positions.

Today, parties litigate because they know of no better alternative. However, as the benefits of mediation become more widely recognized, it will undoubtedly become the most utilized tool for resolving civil disputes in the future.

By: Michael J. Roberts
   A full time professional mediator.
   He has 36 years in the legal profession and has been a mediator since 1985.

Chapter 6

All You Need To Know About Mediation But Didn't Know To Ask- A Parachute For Parties In Litigation!

A recently completed high-rise office building leaks when it rains at the roof, walls, windows and decks. The estimated cost of repair exceeds several million dollars. You're the developer seeking to recover those costs. (You may be general contractor or architectural firm to whom the developer is looking for recovery. Or, you may be one of the two dozen subcontractors and vendors who worked on their project who everyone else is blaming for the leaks.) You have learned that if this claim can be resolved out of court, you could avoid the time and cost of deposing witnesses, preparing for trial, and trial. Depositions, including an army of experts would take 115 days. Preparation for trial and the trial itself would take another 129 days. It would cost close to two million dollars in attorneys fees, expert witness fees and other expenses to recover the several million dollars in repair costs. This dispute clearly has the potential of becoming a living nightmare.

Though parties begin litigation with the expectation of winning, rarely is a case a 'slam dunk' winner. Even "slam dunk winners" have downside risks for both plaintiff and defendant, getting to the point of judgment will likely be extremely expensive in terms of cash outlay, and impact upon the party's emotional, personal and business life. Many difficult and painful questions arise: How much is trial going to cost? What are my realistic chances of success? How do I stop my stomach from churning? Eventually, it dawns on almost every party that it would be nice to settle the dispute before trial. Since 95% of all lawsuits settle before trial, how does one resolve the dispute sooner than later?

Alternatives To Litigation And Trial

Alternatives to litigation and trial are referred to as Alternative Dispute Resolution, or ADR, and include arbitration, court settlement conferences and mediation, among others.

Mediation is a process in which a neutral, called a mediator, assists the parties in exploring issues in the case. The mediator facilitates discussion between counsel and parties, and guides the parties toward finding their own solutions to the dispute. In traditional mediation, the mediator does not make a decision, a court reporter is not present, and there are no rules of evidence which control, the process, with the exception of a rule concerning confidentiality.

Traditional Mediation

There are many forms of mediation. The most commonly used form is traditional mediation. This process has several distinct phases. In the first phase, the joint session, all parties, attorneys and the mediator are present. The parties may choose to have additional persons present, such as experts or psychologists. The attorneys present their client's view of the facts and a discussion of the law which is applicable. It is critical for the parties to personally tell their stories and be heard by the opposing party and attorney.

If the parties listen carefully, they are likely to learn that the opposition's perceptions are starkly different from their own. Becoming aware of these major differences in perceptions of events which led to the dispute is extremely beneficial. When the parties carefully consider their different positions on important issues, they can begin to understand how difficult it will be for a, judge or jury to make a decision. Which party is right? Which party is telling the truth? What proof does each party have to support its claims?

What Role Do The Parties Play In The Mediation?

Each participant in the mediation has a critical role. In fact, if each participant does not play the role the way It needs to be played, the mediation may fail. A party to a dispute or lawsuit needs to participate fully in the mediation process, preferable even before the mediation begins. Each party benefits by helping plan the mediation process, and each needs to help his attorney prepare for the mediation. A party needs to listen very carefully to what the opposing attorney says in his/her opening statement. This is a preview of what the judge or jury will hear during trial. Listen carefully.

Who Must Be Present At The Mediation?

Each party must have a person present who can make a binding decision on behalf of that party. If the party is an individual, he or she must be present. If the party is a corporation, there must be an officer present who can bind the corporation. If the party is a governmental agency, all persons from the agency who are necessary to make a recommendation to the governmental board must be present. If an insurance company is involved, a representative with sufficient authority to make a decision on behalf of the insurance company must be present and represented by someone who can make a binding decision? The dispute will very likely not settle otherwise.

In some cases, parties may wish to have their technical experts at the mediation. When all parties have their experts present, this allows the opportunity to learn more than they would from days of costly experts depositions.

In some disputes, emotional issues are a major, if not controlling, component. Unless the emotional issues are addressed during the joint session and explored during the caucus sessions, the dispute may not settle. Insurance bad faith, wrongful discharge, sexual harassment, and discrimination disputes are usually very highly emotionally charged. In these disputes, it may be very helpful to have his or her psychologist present. For example, in a recent wrongful discharge/malicious prosecution case (without getting too technical, you can assume this type of case is very nasty), during pre-mediation discussions with counsel,

I suggested to plaintiff's attorney that the plaintiff bring her psychologist to the mediation for support. When it came time for the plaintiff to tell her story, she absolutely froze. We adjourned the joint session so I could caucus with the plaintiff, her psychologist and attorney, where she was encouraged to share her story and feelings. When the joint session resumed, though the plaintiff spoke openly, though briefly, as well. The case settled, and I attribute the settlement to the honest and open brief, discussion between the employee and ex-employer.

Preparing For Mediation

Several days before the mediation begins, the attorneys exchange mediation statements. Unlike briefs—which are never brief—mediation statements are summaries of the factual claims and legal arguments. After the mediation statements have been exchanged, the parties and their attorneys will discuss the often glaring strengths in the opposition's position and the weaknesses in their own position. These are risk factors. Each party needs to discuss the risk factors very thoroughly with their attorney and understand them before the mediation begins. This is a good time to begin seriously considering solutions, both monetary and nonmonetary, and how far one can stretch to settle the dispute. Do not wait until the mediation to start thinking about these points. Be creative.

What Are The Costs of Mediation Compared To Trial

Mediation may take several hours, a day, or longer. The length of the mediation depends on the number of parties, the complexity of issues, and how well prepared the parties and their attorneys are. More importantly, the length of the mediation is dependent on how flexible the parties are, and how compelling their desire to resolve the dispute. The cost of mediation is economical compared to the alternatives of trial and what leads up to it. Just one pretrial motion by the attorney may cost more than mediation. Trial is infinitely more expensive, financially and emotionally, and is much riskier than mediation.

What Is The Best Timing For Mediation?

Timing is critical in mediation. The best timing for mediation is as early in the dispute as possible after the parties and attorneys have a very good handle on all the factual and legal issues. Preferably the mediation should take place before expensive discovery, such as depositions, which can become very costly.

Enlightened Judges And Mediators Take The View That Once Depositions Have Begun The Parties Have Already Lost. Why?

By that time, after investing lot of money in the litigation process, parties will have become less flexible and more entrenched in their positions. In fact, as the attorneys become more prepared for trial, the more difficult it is to settle the dispute. If mediation is attempted at this late time, parties ask for recovery of their attorneys fees. The reality is, however, in a negotiated settlement, whether through mediation or otherwise, each party usually pays their own attorney's fees. In addition, parties and attorneys begin to believe that theirs is the only possible "correct", or "righteous" position. Sometimes parties and their attorneys believe that they therefore have nothing to lose by going to trial. This is an unfortunately common and expensive exercise in self-deception. A party can always lose. In trial one party always loses. In multi-party cases, several parties lose. In a successful mediation no one loses.

How Much Time Should You Allow For The Mediation?

Mediation requires patience. It takes time to work through each phase. If the mediation is rushed, parties will feel they have not had an opportunity to be heard. This may cause the mediation to fail. Sometimes it may seem mediation moves slowly. However, as the parties invest more time and energy into the problem solving process, it gains momentum and leads to settlement. It takes time for the parties and counsel to work through the process and for the mediator to learn all the important facts and legal positions. This becomes an investment by everyone so that they cannot easily walk away from the mediation without saying they have failed.

How Do I Get The Opposition To Mediation?

Easy. Have your attorney contact the appropriate mediator who will discuss the possibility of mediation with the opposing attorney. Not only do mediators help parties settle disputes, they can get the parties to the negotiating table.

Documenting The Agreements

Once settlement of the dispute is reached, it should be documented immediately and signed by all parties and counsel. nail it down! If this is not done, there is a risk that the parties will change their minds. Drafting the settlement agreement with the mediator present immediately resolves disputes in language which could otherwise take weeks to resolve.

The Need For Closure And Commitment

So many disputes are fueled by emotion, anger, pain and the desire for "justice". The closest most parties will come to justice is through settlement on terms that they help achieve. Justice will likely not be attained in trial because there is an enormous risk the judge or jury may not see the facts with the same passion or emotion as the party. Therein lies the need for closure, at a point in time the parties can control. Closure in litigation means bringing an end to the grief, constantly churning stomach and great outflow of money which fuels the engines of war. Seize the opportunity!

The mere desire to settle a dispute is not enough. A successful mediation is like a successful relationship. It requires commitment. If all parties and counsel commit to resolving the dispute, there will be a settlement. Mediation is a living process which evolves as a result of the parties' participation in it. When all the ingredients are present, it works phenomenally well.

BY: Paul Fisher
    Has been a mediator and an arbitrator for more than 15 years.

www.ingramcontent.com/pod-product-compliance
Lightning Source LLC
Chambersburg PA
CBHW031553210526
45464CB00003B/1291